What is Essential? Jenny Bates knows well and isn't afraid to tell you with her unique and essential voice. Throughout this wonderful collection, Bates gives voice to those who walk, crawl, swim, and fly in the world with us, our essential partners and common souls. Her eyes report what so many of us miss how "Light mist beads /on a deep blue Sparrow," how plants work beside us and within us (especially in her namesake poem "Creeping Jenny" and in "Drupe Venialis").

These poems are passionate in no way distant or detached but engaged and embracing, celebrating. Bates and her poems are essential because "We are born of a mother that is not / dependent on us. // She is a planet - and a small, fragile / one at that."

Be warned: "A touch dangerous as lightning, / purposeful as a stone placed / in a particular berth."

Then touch this book, open it, read it. It is truly essential.

-Paul Jones, *Something Wonderful*

Essential blends what every human being knows: that instinct rules, as soul never dies, yet survives directions as Fox's feet Jenny Bates settles effortlessly. To read the poems is to camp out among the stars of the universe and to appreciate the little and big creatures in forests of Memory's imagination, for Jenny Bates is custodian of the earth's spirit, that "silence between the beating of wings."

- Shelby Stephenson was poet laureate of North Carolina from 2015-2018. His recent book is *Country*.

Jenny Bates has a well-developed sixth sense and she uses it to feel and observe the natural world. This is a volume by a poet who communicates with the natural world, not simply by listening, but by speaking back. I found evidence of true empathy with non-human creatures in these writings.

- Catherine Raven, author of *Fox & I: An Uncommon Friendship*

"A captivating exploration of the human experience...an exquisite poetic journey that delves deep into the raw essence of existence, urging readers to reconnect with their primal selves with vivid imagery and untethered emotion...the poems explore the fragmented nature of the soul, yearning for unfiltered experiences that nourish and rejuvenate the spirit."

- Roula-Maria Dib, PhD, Director, London Arts-Based Research Centre Founding Editor, Indelible; Creative Producer, Indelible Evenings and Psychreative IAJS, Board of Directors (member)

ALSO BY THE AUTHOR

Opening Doors: an equilog of poetry about Donkeys

Coyote With Coffee

Visitations

Slip

Where the Deer Sleep

ESSENTIAL

poems

Jenny Bates

REDHAWK
PUBLICATIONS

Redhawk Publications
The Catawba Valley Community College Press
2550 Hwy 70 SE
Hickory NC 28602

ISBN: 978-1-959346-19-7

Library of Congress Number: 2023944342

Printed in the United States of America

Interior Design by Ashlyn Blake

Cover Design by Robert Canipe

To every creature, every plant, every tree

Special Thanks

to Catherine Raven and her Fox…What can I say? who teaches us that wild things are safe to love as long as you do not expect it in return. Humans and animals are vulnerable to love, the ruler of all, but not one natural chaotic creature or riotous growth can give you something they don't have to give. Listen to them anyway, because their final words will always be standing there in your dreams, never quite lost or forgotten.

to those who are left unnamed, but who have claimed me none the less as a poet and friend and love me anyway, they continually give me courage and dignity.

I can only quote Ovid in Exile here in my gratitude for …

Sometimes I stop at a word whose precise meaning escapes me for the moment, and I feel fear, the impotence and the rage that the very old feel when their minds start to go, and the tears come… It's a hell of a life, my friend. But I hang in there, singing like a little birdie does — or maybe a crow.

Table of Contents

PART 1
SHADE

PART 2
HEAT

PART 3

RAIN

PART 4

BREEZE

PART 5
CLOUDS

Foreword

Soren Kierkegaard suggests each of us is "to become what one is." Authentic. Which the existentialists further define as "the degree to which a person's actions are congruent with his or her values and desires." Look it up. You'll likely find a picture of Jenny Bates. Trust me. I know of no other poet who is more authentic in word and deed. And in spirit.

She will tell you she's searching for great truth as an animal whisperer to Donkeys, Coyotes, and Crows and that this collection is an invitation to jump on board for the adventure. I suspect however, she already knows the answers and is eagerly waiting for the moment we make the discovery "ourselves." She is the Zen monk pointing at the brilliant moon while simultaneously trying to get out of the way. If you know Jenny, you know she prefers to never be in the picture and will often vanish when the cameras come out—leaving the rest of us posing.

I've watched her stop her own poetry reading and ask members of the audience to embrace a kinder view of vultures. We didn't seem to see the need, so she worked the room like an evangelist until we were all prepared to walk the aisle professing our public conversions. Then back to poems. Natural-like.

With a striking voice that spills over and smooths the edges like clear water, she channels saints from Hildegard to Francis and reassures us the forest can go on forever and there is no line, even a blurry one, between tame and wild. Slither, swim, walk, gallop, fly—we each get there however we can. But it's most fun if we do it together.

It is simplistic to suggest this book is a collection of "nature" poems. These are soul poems, speaking truth plain and pure. Small treasures you get to unwrap and keep—again and again. Surprised for a second or third time by a new and unexpected insight and revelation. But I am mostly struck by the grace within Jenny's words. These are poems of acceptance, and therefore, also poems of healing. And peace. Jenny has never been afraid to touch an open wound or share a symbolic scar. It's okay. Everything is okay. It always has been. Always will be. Just as it is. Just as we are. And you're always good in Jenny's world ... even if you're still wavering on the vulture thing. So yes, I'm sure you'll definitely agree ... it's *Essential.*

David Dixon, *The Scattering of Saints*

Be like the fox who makes more tracks than necessary,
some in the wrong direction.
          Practice resurrection — Wendell Berry

PART 1:
Shade

a Yellow Jacket saved from drowning
in the Water Bowl stung me anyway
any exposed skin, oh yes, they find their
way in

Soul of a ...

Tell me your cellular process

your ancient beating heart is

exhausted by domestication

wild spirit of the earth

be earthy again.

Your soul fragments squawk

to open enliven limbs.

Raw radical unexpected

unrehearsed undiluted experience

thirsty for roots — sense and

senses that feed and quench

the parched stream of spirit.

Underbelly

Show me your wound
the shallow of it

The sensation of mist
hedging your ankles

Cells and blood of seeing
cry deeply —

as I die in your arms

Inform my eye
not the other way around

Show me your painful imagery
so I can believe the scars

That I've never before encountered.

The Road Is Long

Each morning I say *Good Mourning* to the dead.

So, if it's ok with you, and you are alive

I'd like to say *I Love You* instead.

Because my head, hands, and ankles

are wrapped and both I and my words

fall short and because I cannot reveal all that

I mourn or know.

There is no way to articulate a long road with

only one path, a last day — so my ankles,

my head, my hands are wrapped on that road

that pushes me long past every known boundary.

What a Crow remarks upon...or mentions in passing

Inevitable —

To gain my attention
you may become wayward.

No wild animal can be made a fool of —
or can make a fool of himself.

Never self conscious —
Embarrassed, what's that?

Irritably harmless and happy
That's me.

Pleasantly over solicitous perhaps
to Dogs —

their fate being neither wild nor domestic
— a sacrement.

Not a re-penitent,
I'm unable to apologize.

Knowing that being dead
                is apology enough.

Beneath Trees

You can
collect
yourself
beneath trees

fallen bark
from branches

only a
small amount
stripped from cover.

But if you
find you
have found
more

than you
need
store it
in a dark
place, burn
it as
incense

a blend
all your own.

Covert incarnation

I picked up a bird today unmoving in a driveway
Starling it was, bigger than I imagined

Clothed in Rainbow hues of purple, orange
bronze and blue.

I looked in his face — checked out his wings,
his legs.

He could be tired from the commute, or dying.
Eyes a bit rheumy.

I asked him how I could care for his soul?
I don't want to be selfish, but set me off the pavement,

would you?
You will live to a ripe old age, I whispered.

He laughed, told me he fell in love once with a bird
who loved to sleep under the stars.

I hope you find her again, I said.
Thank you for holding me, moving me…

I just wanted to help, to learn who you were
there, not moving.

Starling glimmered in the sun, soaking it up.
I'll hide in the thicket if I need to.

Thank you, I won't forget and I excused myself
with amazement and hope that I am watched

just as closely whenever I go.

Put on hold

Who would not prefer
the open air
beauty of synchronicity
circling your
dying breath
Vultures overhead —
to a beeping
sterile hospital
bed.

Anyone who can see
thermals — is ok by me
my corpse won't get
infected and bacteria won't
spread.

I'll be clean
in balance
from my toes
to my head.

Flight without power
I rise into the sky
windborne on updrafts
levitating and patient
I leave the earth.

But death is not something
you schedule between
vacation and a trip
to the grocery store
and so far,
I've only hinted
to the Vultures I know
to make them
feel good about
what they do
how they look
to us all.

Native legend says
they were so beautiful once —
I tell myself the same —
but then they pushed the sun
away from burning the Earth
lost head and neck
feathers and well, good looks.

By now you must think
I'd like to be eaten by Vultures
like some Native wannabe
so I'll stop in the middle
deny all I've said,
because I'll probably be ashes
to scatter instead.

Your hands an arbor
with no frame or ritual or
wake-up call left.

Persuasion

In my feral state
I can't persuade myself
into anyone's former lover.
My body less punctuated
by another's tracings.

Foxes and Lacewings
feel like a second full Moon.
I'm pearly iridescence not
glorious red glow.

I am the silence between
the beating of wings.

Sen-Sen and Magpies

When my hair turns snow white
I shall let it avalanche, feather on stone

Licorice on clove glistening, shiny
bright with age

Stealing everything it can carry off
tears, patience, tame forgiveness

A wrapped and unguarded limbed
out spruce of hair

Glinting against a blue sky before
it is discontinued

A dissolving pastille of 19th century
Sen-Sen fragrant in your mouth

My hair will light on your fingertips
arm and shoulders as a cluster

Of Chickadees hopes for bread and
cookie crumbs.

The Question

Light mist beads
on a deep blue Sparrow

Stunted with constancy
growing old as though human

Shivering as the trees
rustle with sudden breeze

it pretends not to hear my question

Drawing back into the bark
as a shadow steps into the sun.

PART 2
Heat

Spiderwebs cover the Phoebe's
nest, don't hear their scratchy
calls anymore just the stalwart
Wren, Cuckoo, Hummingbirds

When I become afraid

I picture the two daddy long-legs spiders

that lived for weeks in the hood of Assisi's St. Francis.

He's a statue at the entrance to hallowed

ground in my woods.

He only wears half a face, broken off who knows

when or how.

I liked him better for what was left.

This allowed those spiders to move in a bit deeper.

St. Francis would have liked that.

From dawn to dark, from dark to dawn

I would grow my hair as long as Victoria Falls

at its tips would be droplets of mist

to moisten your face.

I would grow my hair as thick as Rain Forests

at its roots would be soft fingers of mycelium

for you to explore.

I would grow my hair until it decides to stop

vast treetops for you to sit or rope your way

swift as thought

drop like a Hawk, river upstream crossed.

Fly anywhere within my hair and be with

anyone among its lace and branches.

Exile and feelings still within —

remaining large and invisible.

How to Heal at a Distance

goodnight to the street sweepers, the nightwatchman, flame keepers
— Tom Waits

We all have those wounds that will never heal

You died. I died. I left you. You left me.

I found you for someone else. They lost you again.

Leaves close. Books close. Tears flow. Stories end.

All any of us really want is to find our guardian angel

and live again.

Then again…do not despair

You'll find your patch of soul, what you need to make

it grow.

Body, desire, understanding plant them there.

Rest with these final words:

Winter is not bare.

You've just misplaced its boon somewhere.

small flame

I slammed the door
but did not solve the problem.

I wish I were a Bat
quiet during the day

but at night…

of course, I would not want
to smell awful, or get stuck

in a bucket, or someone's hair

really? Terror, I don't care for it.

I don't like fire either, dreadful.
But a small flame — just my size

that would not blind me.

A refuge from the darkness, that's all.
One where I can save time for libation

consume the rest.

Red and Green

where the surface of one thing meets the surface of another… — William Bridges

You were twisting and turning
leaping and swerving a flame

on each foot, on a field so green
so green — so gorgeously

green, the earth's addiction.

And you, warrior Fox as you fought
you fought off the mysterious foe, rattled like

a shaman losing part of his soul.

You danced between spirit and spirit and matter
danced all parts of your body a spontaneous *me!*

When you finally stopped puffing
from chaos, from chaos and glee you flowed

a rhythm of stillness — so still

you stood as if in meditation
and mantra on what you created.

Like a doorbell of being

you called me today
just as the horizon was spent

though you not my Romeo
nor I your Juliet.

I answered this time a welcome
to you, for this is a place that

is your home too.

Your song a small baptism
mine slight in return

I know you can see me —

your rare and precious appearance
smoldering.

It's a remedy to hear you —
sanctuary given to great pain.

It has texture and hope and
a membrane I could loiter in.

But you won't let me yet —
you say it gives it more power

and effect.

You postpone my heart, your
single voice on a cliff a wish-

kindling of memory next morning
still alive and burning.

Drupe Venialis

You fell asleep inside my body

a curled up creature, heart-slowed

yet I could hear, *no — feel* your breath

against my rib cage.

Behind my eyes, on my fingertips

touch-me-not you sang emerging

rays from my pulse, surfacing my skin

a rill, then a flood.

Overflowing my secrets, my seconds,

stems and colors you rushed out

wild on the page.

Afraid, I dropped you, you

disappear — as things tend to do.

Ah, I am a bungler, rubbing my

affected paper skin like an overdue bill.

Safe conduct, immediate relief if —

I can pit, cure, surrender to new moons

and dying stars.

Creeping Jenny

Convolvulus arvensis L.

I am only a wild weedy
Morning-glory.

Perhaps meaner and a bit
more adhesive.

Yet full of winding lap-love
that's due to invade.

Eradicate my withwind
beauty if you must.

I'll twine and bind in
due time.

Not Too Open

Do you smell like goodnight?

Your shape without shape
carries lichen, stone
the musty, damp
rich earth fragrance.

I mantle its touch,
rough salt and wind
piercing my heart
like a quill.
I don't reach up
to pull it out.

Instead, I imagine you
in words soaking
up water when the
time comes.
Trapping my welcome
as I swirl your
lips with starlight.

Essential

Trees are a gathering of circles.

If I touch this tree
say your name,

Light from the moon, the stars
will burn inside it.

Frost kindles its leaves to flame,
spills them on to yellowing grass.

Unchanged.

From prehistoric times the ages
are inconsolable, so they turn.

Mantle shadows by truly seeing
them.

I tell you this as I touch the tree,
circle this tree, say your name.

The tree and its golden mean listen
without an ear to hear.

As you wear yourself out
with a single, essential thought.

Give.

PART 3
Rain

Where are my Crows?
shading in the neighbor's
cow pasture, near the stream
the world in summer goes
belly up to the insects

*The world being illusive, one must be
deluded
in some way if one is to triumph in it*
— *W.B. Yeats*

Wintergreen

Can you hear me? asks the small sturdy plant
at my feet.

Are stones blessed by rain? I answer there and
back again.

*Sometimes, there is great suffering, pain cannot
be explained, sometimes.*

the invisible necessity that has brought you here
you will open like a gift.

a refuge from a call, you wonder what all this
means I expect, from a small

winter plant with an urgency to live.

I felt a Winter Bee today — and tensed with
gentle possibility.

Can you hear me? I asked.

And through its breath faint hum and wing
it strummed and answered back,

Yes.

What we put inside before Winter comes

Punching wind bruising earth's surface

just like grief it filters through hands

cries down acorns, leaves — it's *Goodbye*

to pleasant sounds, the heating of the day.

There will be more knocking on walls

dead silence, voices subdued and tentative

except, the Wren and Crow who always

speak in full pitch restored as the true colors

of Fall — the true dwellings of torment

swallowed then spread on bared ground

from their throats.

Be Bold

I said to the Woodpecker
as I lifted it off the ground
cradled it for a half an hour, this
second Woodpecker to break its neck.

I'm no angel I said to him, though I've
been called it many times
a few drops of Be Bold I tell myself
when there is a need, but sometimes
those drops don't soak in and I'm left
buckling to my knees.

The body will be gone by morning
and sure enough it was, yet still I
struggle How can one keep up with
death stare it in the face? Or program our
unconscious to react in certain ways?

Sweet smelling or dour unpleasant odors
are all we instinctively know, and here,
I'm not too Bold.
I placed the bird on one big leaf, hearing
another drum away
laid his head on dry curled grass
a pine bough for a wreath
both of us changed and changing
the pattern of our resonance.

Wander Everywhere Before You Get There

When I am dead, even then,
I will still love you,
I will wait for you in these poems,
When I am dead, even then
I am still listening to you
I will be making poems for you
out of silence;
silence will be falling into
that silence… —Muriel Rukeyser

Are there things after death? —
surely not.
Though I have been taught,
there is.

You brought me a gift the other night
floated it in a bowl of rain water
like a lotus

A Deer Mouse, you said *for your fear.*

Even then, this morning I saw depressed
empty in leaves
your curled body asleep under my balcony.
You left a note again for me to read,
it began

Human solitude is so very solitary
you must collect every reflection
see me there, my transformation.

I am not defeated, nor are you
in waves again, then again
I come back to you.

Your solitude needs me
a refuge more important than death
its meaning I light as lanterns
in the dark.

In each other as in the stars
guiding to extinction.

As I set the Deer Mouse on top of a boulder,
I said *thank you* to what my soul adores

I returned your gift as the dawn rose from
darkness, strengthened toward noon,
fell away toward evening,
when night returns.

Breathe, Relax, Smile, Spin

especially in the skin of a spider

who decides to rent space within.

Fences, lanterns, strings, bells even

barks won't keep them from getting in.

Out of night air, in numbers they come

from deep in some space or fireplace hum.

Vapory-crawling like delicate lightning

that flickers then vanishes toward a safe

height.

I don't know — why spiders still govern

nameless fear, staying well away from

capturing light.

When no one was looking

actually, I did hear a tree fall in the forest the other night

It echoed once, then split

I found its gaping wound and all nestled by the creek

I checked inside and along its length for little lives

like after an earthquake, to make sure none survived

the fall

this new casualty won't become paper or a hearth fire

only perhaps someone's new home

it will unify its body like the hearth, maybe become a meeting

for wood's gossip or where a Fox could rest his arm

the break looks painful and there were signs of building at the base

twigs carefully crisscrossed and paced with leaf debris

had to have been quite a shock to whoever might have been there

and the creek just rushing by not even a chance to say goodbye

surrounding fellow trees who just hope they can make it through

Winter and see that ecclesiastically this companion — *better him*

than me — didn't

so are trees the heart and keepers of the earth? is their body holy?

harder to tell, when their skin is bare

do they long for their leaves and find more rapture in the wind?

or are they happy to be broken, laying in the arms of their mother

once again.

I listen

to the Scarlet Tanager repeating, repeating, repeating
weaving his avian poesy of sound, a supplication full
of time and energy graceful, graceful, graceful living
from the world

it never stops, never stops his bombardment the same
the same, all the same bombardment of phrase, a weapon
weapon, a handful of pliancy

I clip

trim I loathe to clip, clip the tendrils, newly reaching
tendrils of wisteria their being there, a coalition of wild
state and native attitude

death within hours, hours of death debates in the woods

I nick

wiry tight whisker, white tight whisker the Raccoon left
at the feeding bowl, my discretion, discretion as false
as hers guerrilla campaign, campaign of commitment
war of nerves, nerve to never spend one minute ironing
curtains to hang in my windows.

Jenny Bates

Antitoxin

Feather tor
Vixen shoal
Heartbeat of a Swan

I don't know how this immunity works,
only that is does work.

It won't wear off, variant empty cast-off
skin of a Snake.

Onion paper
Light dry
Small breeze booster

Thistledown, bent once again to earth.

Born From the Hand

staring at dawn
and ending as dusk

I bob up and down
in place

can't explain any deep
meaning for this.

a vernal point something
mentioned

earlier by Ptolemy in
the second century perhaps.

did Christ do this too?
this centering of initiate

did he look out to space?
so to speak?

mystery of Golgotha
already taken place

and I oscillate
prostrate looking back

in time to the turning
point of time.

Christ performed an
earthly deed I think.

Like the streaming
of music under that

piece of sky —
must be the same whether

we label it transformate
this or eucharist that.

he was a farmer
ploughing his field with a

Mule under an
etheric tableau in tune with

seeds, dirt, the sun in hand
baptism by rain.

PART 4

Breeze

*You don't know when
another sting will find
you, I go out anyway
just to blend in, wearing
my shirt with a Tiger on
it — no one questions
Tigers*

Quest for Dragons

All the trees that were lost last winter

pines they were, their fallen branches

litter the back road a spine three inches

deep.

They look like the bones and teeth shed

from a Dragon soaking into the ground

they lay earth bound.

No subject to wind, or bird nor raccoon

claw, they will mind their own business

watching, waiting until the others fall.

That storm uprooted the old hood of a

car gripped for years to a tree brought

down.

Up it stands by a Dragon's breath

resurrecting its world from a forgotten

body of bruise and rust.

No Dragon hoard

of gold and music

gems and wishes

flowers and gardens

of reincarnation carried on long

sinuous necks.

Return Once More

Wings folded, I can't decide
should I fly?

I stretch them out slow —
still connected.

I clean them meticulously
form them for flight.

I spell it out for them
the logistics of air, wind, cloud.

They ruffle in return, vibrating
with anticipation.

*Will we have boundless luck
today?* they ask.

Perhaps not today, I say back.

They droop, spread out tip
to ground.

Making not a sound as I lift
them into place.

Tucked close to my breast
treat them with the greatest respect.

How We Sing

the Coyotes on the mountain sing
like they are stitching a wound

the Deer snort and run as one
eyes wide and tails up in retreat

four maybe more voices brake
the dusk the sludge of day

into four pieces cast each piece
in four directions declaring

something with each throw in
a language I did not know

but that felt deeply comforting
to me.

when we form a relationship
with our God do we sing to Him?

deciding to Live letting Him know
through this outward gesture

of song?

those Coyote voices snap my
soul like a rubber band

eerie quartet of the invisible
for no matter how I stared

waited for movement on the
hillside I never saw them

I only knew I had stopped
breathing as long as they

were singing a song older than
the beginning

that night before I lay down
to sleep all I could do was

lean my head against the
windowsill and whisper.

Moth Voices

The last sunset of summer
squeezing on the rim, an aging
eye closing.

Fox's giggling begins
out of his mouth, into the
huddling dusk.

Moths swarm then scatter
taking their voice —
a diaphanous flutter.

Fox coughed as one came late
in his throat, then left unharmed,
uncaught into a breeze.

It was large and beautiful
as it spread its never blinking eyes
back to Fox.

With breath like clove, lemons
crushed with rose, it rose and wrote
—for it had no mouth.

Fox was heady, warmth and sweetness
potent and greeting, a thin thought
he smelled of frankincense paused the air...

Just, Moth song began,
sacrifice and death forced from
the land, but sorrow none

Our time has come to
reach and leap for the stars!
...still laughing, that Fox.

When a Vulture dies

      his shadow becomes a slamming door

his friends soar

      then paw with claw over his dumping.

He becomes a skid-row bum

      holding up a V for victory

to passing caterpillars, fringed gentians

      field mice.

Poet to Poet

I don't stay long in cultivated soil

it is a torture to endure.

Straight rows and hedges, gardens

with ledges are anguish.

Give me a wild morning scattered,

overgrown and pesty

moonbeam grown woodbine

and oh, so common, poet to poet

weeds.

Where soil is deep

inclined to be heavy, wet and

rich with violin music from

fiddle shaped leaves.

It makes little difference to me,

check the underside of my pad

my veins smile with the same

depth you place your lamented

dead.

All Experience Comes to You

I arrived back home smelling faintly of Skunk
a whiff of Opossum

no one noticed.

Unlike the dead I found I could not give them
vacancy

I unclenched their hands, they were hands,
from shock

Unwrapping each finger, carefully. They had
fingers, with nails, pads and whorls like mine

I tell them I'm sorry I cannot wed my lips
to words of waking or make

them breathe again.

The Opossum wasn't faking —
the Skunk never had a chance

I tell them softly that they were just
what I wanted today

in case they thought the car that hit them
said the same.

A few thoughts on archery

to

the calf born yesterday shivering in the field with
no shelter and no more notice by the ground that

it lays on

sacred bloody yard art that may grow up anyway
to become someone's afternoon meal.

So

I'm a bit skeptical today, for what I see is a
beautiful stream of calf music, a flowing of life
that lives in accordance with itself and its world.

Not

for my altering to interfere.

You

may think me a nut on one of those trees
up there in your everywhere, that's ok.
I'm wounded just like you.

I'll

continue to be like Artemis with a quiver
full of soul arrows, my life a bow aiming at you
because there is nothing that you have not been —

me too.

Foxlight

legend has it that Foxes carry the aurora on the tip of their tails

I try to catch it, the light tipped at the end of your tail.

My clumsy trembling approach from behind

crackles a twig —

    swift and silent, you are gone.

This time, I hold on!

Get myself flung across the sky behind a new tree

blossoming green ghostly leaves in a wind storm.

You tunnel through the air as if it were ground.

I sit empty handed once again, an earthbound

crisscrossed jumble.

My bulk dropped off to dust, lost to the debris of

forest floor.

Better Than Windows

How to describe the hope that lingers in memory?

Is it the howl of one Grey Wolf? or perhaps the fragrance

of a single flower of White Clover notching the heart

after the world continues its slobbering.

Those nicks, never made out of place, gentle

as a Crow shooing away a Chipmunk becomes a game.

Let the world drool.

Every lament, sweet smell opens one of the sutures.

PART 5
Clouds

Wood Thrush dances
delicately on the railing
as I write, timbre and bell–
clear voice of this shy
bird is better than any choir
I walk outside again,
hearing the constant insect
thrum just below the surface
of sight

Auras

the days I can't find you are hard

the nights even worse

tend the soul, even charm to

make it more desirable

lift it to enchantment

nurse life along I say

sometimes the train arrives on time

sometimes, a faltering therapy

because God seems to prefer a good stroll

walking together with God —

try walking with a hurricane or

deep reverberation of snow.

Clouded Leopard

How does it feel returning from extinction?

Climbing head first down
my Anthropocene spine

I break, with each twist of
wrist, incision of claw.

Divergent several million years
reduced to eleven in captivity.

Under your limber bones
I squall, choke and pitch
tip into your patient wound.

Wind your tail round my neck
hero of revenge, and ossified
purr.

Your long tooth guilt-piercing.
We won't say anything to anyone
perilous beauty kills.

Shroud me in your cloud.

Planetary Tracing

Red-Tailed Hawk's cry sheers the sky
like a child carefully cutting out a cloud.

Stay in the lines! the Hawk wails
his wings oiling, tracing the air.

You know by his voice, this Hawk listens
to planets, plants, stones, and animals.

Severing carefully, reducing life to
fundamentals, free of drudge and contemplation.

Scaling the earth with spread of wing
flirting his patch he strings, threads sunlight

Faltering the first streaks of dawn.

Unfold

Crow take my eyes

Bear my tracks

Coyote unfasten my tell

Cotton Rats and scat

Meadow Voles untried

unfit up-awing uproar

take me up-in-to the air

between talons of Falcon

Eagle and sker

I'm up for grabs

in unborn fecund silence.

Owl dream me

here in this crowded

hearth of Soul

Every night I let you go

one of a gallery an unhinged

collection that belongs

together yet hangs on various

walls.

Fox shelter me until I'm tied

and undefined in your jaws.

When an Osprey

with the stillness of a bee on your hand
you said hunting for my eyes

it took twenty years to get over you

we have a place now, I repeated your
words silently I prayed like lightning

who am I to doubt the dead

but I am slow to learn, hungry though
there is food all around

like a supple young shoot growing near
a rock

a struggling fish breaking its neck in your
grasp

the bee becoming all I see delivering me
still and hung on the grey turrets of trees

by an Osprey

I allow myself some confusion dangling
there

until I own the slight your laughter wind
whipped

slashing my skin with moonlight.

On the page

How long can we hold our breath?

Keep time with being behind schedule

    What

is a schedule anyway except a way

to disturb presence

Each encounter becoming memory

To be above all the weather of the world

    Depth

digesting drop disappearing allowing

my touch to come through on the page.

The Meaning

Don't look for me now

he said

or wait

I said that once

on a page

but your missing

I said

or wait

you said you

miss me?

Please,

don't open those soft

enlivened eyes

not yet.

You have many shapes

to leave me

and I

have many other places

in which I

dwell.

Ash Wednesday

Grateful not far from great fall I say as I forget
to fast today with the sky full of prescribed burning
and mist.

I'd like to be on the Tibetan plateau right now
pondering Nietzsche, or Buddha or Christ I don't
know, with a big Blue Bear.

Ursus arctos pruinosus is the third Spirit Bear
ever created. He can run the gamut of the color
spectrum.

How about you? they say he holds the days
as I would hold him in good weather.
New levels of awareness there I bet.

I would like a face looking back at me
instead of fear that we don't want to be
that we don't want to see.

Tells me where I need to go because it is a
place that will make us stronger.

One I would have known eventually even as
I only stare at Himalayan salt with a label
that makes me reach for the summit.

Eventually, I would have known there is
solace, peace and a sense of home at the
end of the journey.

Holding

You said to me, *If you were to hold*
my hand in both of your hands as greeting,
you would panic.

A touch dangerous as lightning,
purposeful as a stone placed in
a particular berth.

Taking something from the Air
and burying it beneath Earth.

An expanding touch, sure to come
into your life as that of insect or weed.

Now, picture a dog who stops staring
at the sky, and looks at you.

If I take your hand in my hands, I mean
it like the yarrow plant finding Achilles
after that arrow struck.

A river flowing from the tip of a
Hummingbird's tongue.

The timeless and protective zone of
evening filled with blue, violet and
miracle.

Well, you said, *if anyone can pull it off,*
you can.

Conceived and Born

There's no suckling here

as though we were

going to get some anyway

The sanctity of Earth is a fast.

The holy presence of prayer a fast.

We are born of a mother that is not
dependent on us.

She is a planet — and a small, fragile
one at that.

ACKNOWLEDGMENTS

Much gratitude for the following publishers of these poems included in this book

Self Educating Poets Network 2021: "Clouded Leopard"

WFDD Inaugural Poetry Collection 2022: "Sen-Sen and Magpies"

London Arts-Based Research Center, Science and Sensibility Issue No 7 2023: "Foxlight"

Weymouth Center for the Arts & Humanities, ExperieNCe Poetry 2023:
"The Question"

Special thanks to layout designer Ashlyn Blake, *who truly made my collection visually come to life.*

BIO

Jenny Bates, member Winston-Salem Writers,NC Poetry Society, NC Writers Network. She has five books, *Opening Doors: an equilog of poetry about Donkeys, Coyote with Coffee* purchased by Vanderbilt and the University of Vermont. *Visitations, Slip, and Where the Deer Sleep.* Published in numerous journals including **NCPS' Pinesong** and **W-S Writers** *Flying South.* Also a decade long poet for **PIPS.** On the 100th Anniversary of WWI, she was asked to help launch poetry dedicated to the history and contributions of Donkeys and Mules during WWI. These poems are now archived for the Animals in War memorial in London. In 2023 she was accepted as a presenter in Kew Gardens, London for the Ecopoetics and Environmental Aesthetics Conference presented by the London Arts-Based Research Centre.

Made in the USA
Columbia, SC
04 September 2023

22397346R00048